After Dinner

Jokes and Funny Stories f

Compiled by Hugh Morrison

Montpelier Publishing
London
2015

ISBN-13:978-1505859003
ISBN-10:150585900X
Published by Montpelier Publishing, London.
Printed by Amazon Createspace.

AGE

'Johnny,' said his mother. 'Please run across the street and see how old Mrs. Brown is this morning.'

'Alright,' replied Little Johnny, and a few minutes later he returned and reported:

'Mrs. Brown says it's none of your business how old she is.'

'You must not talk all the time, dear,' said the mother who had been interrupted.

'When will I be old enough to, mummy?' asked the little girl.

Little Johnny was sitting on his grandfather's knee one day. After looking at him intently for a time he said:

'Grandpa, were you in the ark?'

'Certainly not,' answered the astonished old man.

'Then why weren't you drowned?'

'To what do you attribute your great age, Mr Smith?' asked a newspaper interviewer of a centenarian.

'Being born a long time ago,' the old gentleman replied.

ARCHITECTS

Everyone is an architect until there's a problem. Then the architect's to blame!

A man was flying in a hot air balloon and realised he was lost. He reduced altitude and spotted a man below. He lowered the balloon further and shouted: 'Excuse me, can you tell me where I am?'

The man below said 'Yes, you're in a hot air balloon, hovering about 30 feet above this field.'

The balloonist said with some irritation: 'You must be an architect.'

'I am' replied the man, surprised with his deduction. 'But how did you know?'

'Because everything you have told me is technically correct, but it doesn't do me any good' said the balloonist.

The man on the ground laughed, 'Well, then, you must be a building contractor.'

'I am' replied the balloonist, "but how did you know?'

'Well' said the architect, 'you don't know where you are, or even where you are going, but you expect me to be able to help you. Now you're still in the same predicament you were in before we met, but now it's my fault.'

Why are architects banned from heaven?

Jesus was a carpenter.

BANKERS

Investment banker (to junior partner): 'There's a thousand pounds gone from one of our accounts - you and I were the only people who had access to it.'

Junior partner: 'Well, suppose we each pay 500 pounds and say no more about it.'

A banker was giving advice to his son who was about to set out into the world of finance.

'Son,' said the father, 'I desire to impress one thought upon your mind: Honesty is always the best policy.'

'Yes, father,' said the young man.

'And, by the way,' added the old man, 'I would advise you to read up a little on company law. It might surprise you to discover how many things you can do in banking and still be honest.'

Johnny had a savings bank;
Made from a biscuit tin.
He passed it round among the boys,
Who put their pennies in.

Then Johnny wrecked that bank and bought
Sweets and chewing gum.
And to the other envious kids
He never offered some.

'What will we do?' his mother said:
'Administer a spanking?'
'No, no,' his father said; 'We'll cultivate
'His gift for modern banking!'

The directors of an investment bank were having their Christmas dinner in the West End. One of them appeared worried during the progress of the meal, and finally he was asked as to the cause.

'I just realised that I forgot to lock the safe before I left the office,' he replied.

'Why worry?' said another member of the firm. 'We're all here.'

A City banker lost his job and told his friend how he set up his own bank.

'Well,' he said, 'I didn't have much else to do, so I rented an empty shop and painted 'bank' on the window. The first day I was open for business a man came in and deposited a thousand pounds with me ; the second day another man dropped in and deposited two thousand; and by about the third day I got so much confidence in the bank that I put in a thousand myself!'

'Yes, sir,' said the trust fund manager, proudly, 'I am the architect of my own fortune.'

'Well,' rejoined the friendly critic, 'all I've got to say is that it's a lucky thing for you there were no building inspectors around when you were constructing it.'

A man wanted to open a new bank account so visited his local branch. Knowing he would have to identify himself, he showed his driving licence.

'Have to see more than one form of identification,' said the clerk.

The stranger took a bunch of utility bills from his pocket all addressed to the same name on his licence.

The clerk shook his head.

The man thought a minute and showed him his watch, which had his name engraved on the back.

But the clerk still refused.

'Those things don't prove anything,' he said.

'But I've given you proof that would convict me of murder in any court in the land.'

'That's probably very true,' responded the clerk, patiently, 'but in matters connected with the bank we have to be more careful.'

'You say that City banker confessed everything? What did he get, five years?'

'No, fifty thousand pounds. He confessed to a publicist.'

BUILDERS

Proud housewife (to visiting builder): 'Please take care on the laminate. I've just had it installed.'

Builder: 'Thanks love but I won't slip – I've got spikes on me boots'

A builder, while carrying a ladder through a crowded street had the misfortune to break a shop window. He immediately dropped his ladder and broke into a run, but he had been seen by the shopkeeper, who dashed after him in company with several salesmen, and was soon caught.

'Here you!' shouted the angry shopkeeper, when he had regained his breath. 'I saw you break my window!'

'I did,' admitted the builder, 'but didn't you see me running home to get the money to pay for it?'

Man: I want some of that tarmac that soaks up water.

Builder's merchant: you mean some of our porous tarmac?

Man: No, I want the best!

A builder sent to make some repairs in a large Kensington house entered the bedroom of the lady of the house with his apprentice and began to work.

'Mary,' the lady said to a servant, 'see that my jewel-case is locked up at once!'

The builder understood. He removed his wallet from his pocket and his watch from his wrist in a significant manner and handed them to his apprentice.

'Sid,' said he, 'take these right back to the van. It seems that this house isn't safe.'

BUSINESS

'I see shares took a drop.'

'Took a drop? It looks more like they took the whole bottle.'

When an East End businessman bought an insurance policy for his factory, the insurer told him he would have to make his first payment immediately.

'How much will it be?' he asked.

'A hundred pounds,' replied the insurer.

'I've got no cash on me just now,' said the businessman. 'Can't you just deduct it from what you'll owe me when the factory burns down?'

'You say you have good references?'

'Yes, over a hundred.'

'And how long have you been a secretary?'

'Two years.'

'Why is it you never get to the office on time in the morning?' demanded the boss angrily.

'It's like this, boss,' explained the tardy one, 'you kept telling me not to watch the clock during office hours, and I got so I didn't watch it at home either.'

'I met your husband today and he was telling me that he is in love with his work.'

'Was he, indeed? I must take a look in at the office.'

A small businessman was getting very behind in settling his debts with suppliers.

They sent him letter after letter, each more politely threatening than the last. Finally they sent their representative down to give him a sporting chance.

'Now,' said the caller,' we must have a settlement. Why haven't you sent us anything? Are things going badly?'

'No. Everything's going splendidly. You needn't worry. My bankers will guarantee me all right.'

'Then why haven't you paid up?'

'Well, you see, those threatening letters of yours were so well done that I've been copying them and sending them round to a few customers of my own who won't pay up, and I've collected nearly all outstanding debts. I was only holding back because I felt sure there must be a final letter, and I wanted to get the series complete.'

'We need brains in this business, young man.'

'I know you do. The business shows it.'

A teacher was trying to explain the dangers of overwork to one of the smaller pupils.

'Now, Johnny,' she pursued, 'if your father were busy all day and said he would have to go back to the office at night, what would he be doing?'

'That's what mum wants to know.'

Doctor: 'Did you try the simple plan of counting sheep for your insomnia?'

Businessman: 'Yes, doctor, but I made a mess of it. I counted ten thousand sheep, put them in a lorry and shipped them to the market. And when I'd got through counting the money I got for them at present prices it was time to get up.'

'Can you let me off to-morrow afternoon? My wife wants me to go shopping with her.'

'Certainly not. We are much too busy.'

'Thank you very much, sir. You are very kind!'

A successful businessman tells the following story about the beginning of his professional life: 'I had just installed myself in my office,' he said,' had put in a phone and had preened myself for my first client who might come along when, through the glass of my door I saw a shadow. Yes, it was doubtless someone to see me. Picture me, then, grabbing the nice, shiny receiver of my new phone and plunging into an imaginary conversation.

It ran something like this: 'Yes, Mr. S.,' I was saying as the stranger entered the office, 'I'll attend to that corporation matter for you. Mr. J. had me on the phone this morning and wanted me to go into partnership, but I had to put him off, as I was too busy with orders. But I'll manage to sandwich your order in between the others somehow. Yes. Yes. All right. Goodbye.' Being sure, then, that I had duly impressed my prospective client, I hung up the receiver and turned to him. 'Excuse me, sir,' the man said, 'but I'm from the telephone company. I've come to connect your phone.'

'Sir, this is a golden opportunity! Small investment, no risk, and enormous returns absolutely sure.'

'Then I wouldn't have the heart to deprive you of it.'

'I can't keep the visitors from coming in,' said the office boy, dejectedly, to the chief executive. 'When I say you're out they just say they must see you.'

'Well,' said the chief executive, 'just tell them that's what they all say.'

That afternoon there called at the office a young lady. The boy assured her it was impossible to see the chief executive.

'But I'm his wife,' said the lady.

'Oh, that's what they all say,' said the boy.

Boss (to office cleaner) 'I'm tired of your carelessness. Just look at that dust on the desks. It's six weeks old at the very least.'

Cleaner: 'Don't blame me, I've only worked here three weeks.'

New cleaner: 'I hope the work's not too hard. In my last job I took things easy.'

Old cleaner: 'Well it's different here. They keep everything locked up.'

CARS

Every normal man has two great ambitions. First, to own his home. Second, to own a car to get away from his home.

After ten years of trouble free motoring, a businessman's Jaguar broke down so he took it to a local garage. The mechanic sucked his teeth and looked doubtful.

'I don't like this model' he said.

'Why, do they break down often?' asked the man.

'No, they hardly ever do.'

CHILDREN

Little Johnny: 'Dad.'

Father: 'Well, what is it?'

Little Johnny: 'It says here, "A man is known by the company he keeps". Is that true?'

Father: 'Yes, I suppose so.'

Little Johnny: 'Well, if a good man keeps company with a bad man, is the good man bad because he keeps company with the bad man, or is the bad man good because he keeps company with the good man?'

CLERGY

'My sermon on austerity made a tremendous impression on the congregation.'

'How do you know?'

'I've just counted the collection.'

The minister of a Methodist church noticed that old Tom, an impoverished pensioner, hadn't attended services for a couple of weeks. Concerned for the old man, the minister visited him at home and asked if he hadn't been to church because he'd been ill.

'It's not that, reverend' said the old man, who answered the door in his pyjamas. 'It's just that I tore me only suit, and I've nothing to go out in'

The minister thought for a moment then remembered that someone had donated a beautiful tailored suit for the church jumble sale. He decided he would donate this to Tom, who accepted it later that day.

The next Sunday, Tom still didn't turn up for church. With growing concern, the minister visited him again.

'Wasn't the suit any good?' asked the clergyman.

'Oh there's nowt wrong with the suit, Reverend.'

'So why weren't you in church?'

'Oh I was, Reverend. The fact is, when I put that suit on, I looked so respectable I decided to join the Church of England.'

Vicar: 'The Bible tells us we should love our neighbours.'

Parishioner: 'Yes, but the Bible was written before our neighbours lived so close'.

A good looking priest found the young ladies in the church rather too interested in him. At last it became so embarrassing that he left. Not long afterwards he met the priest who had succeeded him.

'Well,' he asked, 'how do you get on with the ladies?'

'Oh, very well indeed,' said the other. 'There is safety in numbers, you know.'

'Ah!' was the instant reply. 'I only found it in Exodus.'

'I understand your vicar has gone to the Holy Land for a month.'

'Yes, that's right.'

'For a holiday, I suppose?'

'Yes, the bishop decided that we were entitled to one.'

A prison chaplain was asked by some of the prisoners to pray for Annie Power. Willingly and gladly he did so for three Sundays in the prison chapel. On the fourth Sunday one of the felons told him he need not do it anymore.

'Why,' asked the good man, with an anxious look, 'is she dead?'

'Oh, no,' said the convict – 'she won the Grand National last week.'

A Sunday-school teacher had been telling her class of little children about crowns of glory and heavenly rewards for good people.

'Now, tell me,' she said, at the close of the lesson, 'who will get the biggest crown?'

There was silence for a minute or two, then a bright little chap piped up :

'Him wot's got t' biggest 'ead.'

A prominent atheist academic was the guest of honour at an Oxford college dinner. Just before the meal commenced, the Dean leant over to him and explained that it was strict college tradition to say Grace before eating.

Since the chaplain was off sick, it was also college tradition that the duty should then fall to the principal speaker. Not wishing to be rude, but acutely aware of his reputation, the academic rose to his feet and solemnly declared:

'There being no clergyman present, let us thank God.'

A stern priest in old Ireland had issued to his people a command against dancing, believing it to be a device of the devil. A few of the young people disobeyed and attended a dance given at a neighbouring town. Finally it reached the ears of the priest, and, meeting one of the culprits on the street one morning, he said in a stern voice:

'Good morning, child of the devil!'

'Good morning, father!' smilingly answered the girl.

A country vicar became increasingly annoyed with the high prices charged in the village shop. One day he reproved the shopkeeper by quoting the Scripture. 'The first shall be last and the last shall be first.'

'It makes no difference to me how you arrange 'em,' replied the tradesman. 'I'm just the middleman'.

A Methodist minister was invited to one of the royal chapels to preach.

'Do you wish to wear a surplice?' asked the chaplain.

'I am a Methodist. What do I know about surplices? All I know about is a deficit!'

The clergyman's eloquence may have been at fault, still he felt annoyed to find that an old gentleman fell asleep during the sermon on two consecutive Sundays. So, after service on the second week, he told the boy who accompanied the sleeper that he wished to speak to him in the vestry.

'Johnny, who is that elderly gentleman you attend church with?'

'Grandpa,' was the reply.

'Well,' said the clergyman, 'if you will keep him awake during my sermon, I'll give you fifty pence each week.'

The boy fell in with the arrangement, and for the next two weeks the old gentleman listened attentively to the sermon.

The third week, however, found him soundly asleep.

The vexed clergyman sent for the boy and said: 'I am very angry with you. Your grandpa was asleep again today. Didn't I promise you fifty pence a week to keep him awake?'

'Yes,' replied little Johnny, 'but grandpa now gives me a pound not to disturb him.'

An Irishman and a Jew were arguing. Finally the subject came round to their respective religions.

'I bet my priest knows more than your Rabbi,' the Irishman insisted.

'Of course he does' replied the Jew. 'You tell him everything.'

'Father,' said the minister's son, 'my teacher says that 'collect' and 'congregate' mean the same thing. Do they?'

'Perhaps they do, my son.' said the venerable clergyman; 'but you may tell your teacher that there is a vast difference between a congregation and a collection.'

A Catholic priest preached a fine sermon on married life and its beauties. Two old Irishwomen were heard coming out of church commenting on the address.

"Tis a fine sermon his Reverence would be after giving us,' said one to the other.

'It is, indade,' was the quick reply, 'and I wish I knew as little about the matter as he does.'

Minister: 'You should be careful! Don't you know that drink is mankind's worst enemy?'

McTavish: 'Yes; but aren't we supposed tae love our enemies?'

CLUBS

A lady rang up her husband's London club and asked to speak to him.

'Your husband isn't here, ma'am,' said the attendant, blandly.

'My goodness!' the lady exclaimed, 'How do you know my husband isn't at the club when I haven't even told you my name?'

The attendant answered more blandly than ever: 'Nobody's husband is ever at the club, ma'am.'

A story is told of a very grand Victorian peer who used to walk home each day from the House of Lords to his house in St James'. On the way he often felt the 'call of nature' and used to stop at the Athenaeum Club to use the facilities. After some months, a club servant noticed this and decided to challenge the gentleman.

'Are you a member, sir?' he asked, politely.

'Good God,' replied the peer. 'Do you mean to say this is a club as well?'

COMMUTING

Ticket collector on London Underground (in summer) 'your ticket's expired.'

Passenger: 'I'm not surprised, in this heat.'

A commuter train was slowly working its way out of London during one of those periods of chaos caused by an inch of snow. Finally it came to a dead stop and all efforts to start it again were futile.

In the wee, small hours of the morning a weary commuter, numb from the cold and the cramped position in which he had tried to sleep, blew on his hands until they were warm enough to send a text message to his boss, which read:

'Will not be at office to-day. Not home yesterday yet.'

Passenger (to London bus driver): 'Can't you go faster than this?'

Driver: 'Yes, but I have to stay with the bus.'

'I left my money at home,' said the lady on the train to the ticket inspector. 'You will have to trust me. I am one of the directors' wives.'

'I am sorry, madam,' replied the inspector. 'I can't do that, even if you were the director's only wife.'

A small boy, who was sitting next to a very haughty woman in a crowded train, kept sniffling in a most annoying way, until the woman could stand it no longer.

'Boy, have you got a handkerchief?' she demanded.

The small boy looked at her for a few seconds, and then in a dignified tone, came the answer.

'Yes, I 'ave, but I don't lend it to strangers.'

'What's wrong now?' asked the impatient passenger to the ticket inspector on a commuter train.

'A cow on the track.'

'But I thought you drove it off.'

'We did,' said the guard, 'but we caught up with it again.'

CRIME

Judge: 'The police say that you and your wife had some words.'

Defendant: 'I had some, but I didn't get a chance to use them.'

A judge asked a woman her age.

'Thirty,' she replied.

'You've given that age in this court for the last three years.'

'Yes. I'm not one of those who says one thing today and another thing tomorrow.'

A policeman rose in court to testify against a prisoner.

'What is this man charged with?' the magistrate demanded.

'Bigotry, yeronner,' the policeman answered. 'He's got three wives.'

'Three!' cried the magistrate. 'That's not bigotry. That's trigonometry!'

'Do you mean to say a physical wreck like your husband gave you that black eye?' asked the magistrate to a complaining wife.

'Yes yeronner, only he wasn't a physical wreck till after he gave me the black eye.'

The prosecuting barrister had encountered a somewhat difficult witness. Finally he asked the man if he was acquainted with any of the people on the jury.

'Yes, sir,' announced the witness, 'more than half of them.'

'Are you willing to swear that you know more than half of them?' demanded the lawyer.

'If it comes to that, I'm willing to swear that I know more than all of them put together.'

A jury recently met to inquire into a case of suicide. After sitting through the evidence, the twelve jurors retired, and, after deliberating, returned with the following verdict:

'The jury are all of one mind — temporarily insane.'

'You are charged with selling adulterated milk,' said the judge.

'Your Honour, I plead not guilty.'

'But the evidence shows that it is 25 per cent water.'

'Then it must be high-grade milk,' returned the plaintiff. 'If your Honour will look up the word 'milk' in your dictionary you will find that it contains from 80 to 90 per cent water. I should have sold it as cream!'

Prison visitor: 'Poor man! What are you locked up here for?'

Prisoner (wearily): 'I suppose they think I'd get out if I wasn't.'

Many years ago a good for nothing fellow was up before the judge for being drunk and disorderly.

'Since this is not your first offence I sentence you to a month in prison with hard labour', said the judge.

'I demand clemency for my husband!' shouted the man's wife from the gallery.

The judge looked up angrily.

'Madam, one month is the minimum time your husband must serve in prison'.

'I'm not asking you to shorten the sentence, yeronner' replied the woman. 'I'm asking if he can do the hard labour at home instead.'

Police inspector (to new recruit): 'If you were ordered to disperse a mob, what would you do?'

Recruit: 'Pass around a hat, sir.'

CULTURE

Sweeping his long hair back with an impressive gesture the visitor faced the Hollywood movie mogul. 'I would like get a job in the movies,' he said.

'You are an actor?' asked the film man.

'Yes.'

'Had any experience acting without audiences?'

A flicker of sadness shone in the visitor's eyes as he replied:

'Acting without audiences is what brought me here!'

After seeing a new play starring a well known actress, a theatre critic praised the leading lady for her performance.

'Madam, you played your part splendidly. It fits you to perfection.'

'I'm afraid not. A young and pretty woman is needed for that part,' said the smiling thespian.

'But, madam, you have positively proved the contrary.'

The great pianist Rachmaninoff told a story about his boyhood.

'When I was a very little fellow,' he said, 'I played at a reception at a Russian count's, and, for an urchin of seven, I flatter myself that I swung through Beethoven's *Kreutzer Sonata* pretty successfully.

'The *Kreutzer*, you know, has in it several long and impressive rests. Well, in one of these rests the count's wife, a motherly old lady, leaned forward, patted me on the shoulder, and said:

'Play us something you know, dear.'

DEATH

The widow of a well-known man, requested that the words 'My sorrow is greater than I can bear' be placed upon the marble slab of her dear departed.

A few months later the lady returned and asked how much it would cost her to have the inscription removed and another substituted.

'No need of that, missus,' replied the mason, soothingly; 'you see, I left just enough room to add 'alone.'

Little Johnny: 'Dad!'

Father: 'Well, my son?'

Little Johnny: 'I took a walk through the cemetery today and read the inscriptions on the tombstones.'

Father: 'And what did it make you think about?'

Little Johnny: 'I wondered where all the bad people were buried.'

A nagging wife finally drove her henpecked husband to an early grave. Feeling lonely with nobody to browbeat, she decided to try to contact her late spouse using a ouija board.

With trepidation in her voice, she asked 'are you there, Albert?'

After a pause, the glass moved and spelt out the message: 'YES'

'Are you in the next world?' asked the widow.

The answer came back. 'YES'

'And are you at peace?'

'YES'

The widow became increasingly curious and asked another question.

'Please tell me what Heaven looks like.'

Slowly the reply was spelt out.

'WHO SAID ANYTHING ABOUT HEAVEN?'

They say that as you get older, you find yourself thinking more and more about the Hereafter. It's true – the other day I walked into this very room and then said to myself 'I can't remember what I'm here after'.

In London's Highgate Cemetery there is a stone, erected by a widow to her loving husband, bearing this inscription: 'Rest in peace - until we meet again.'

An epitaph in an old Suffolk graveyard read:

Remember, friend, as you pass by,
As you are now, so once was I;
As I am now thus you must be,
So be prepared to follow me.

Afterwards, some wag added in pencil:

To follow you I'm not content
Till I find out which way you went.

Another gravestone inscription:

Here lies Maria Brown,
Wife of Timothy Brown,
aged 80 years.
She lived with her husband fifty years, and died
in the confident hope of a better life.

In an English country churchyard:

Here lies the body of Enoch Holden, who died suddenly and
unexpectedly by being kicked to death by a cow.

'Well done, thou good and faithful servant.'

DOCTORS

A country GP received a call from an anxious patient on a remote farm who was suffering from fever with a high temperature. He demanded the doctor visit him immediately.

'You must give me a thermometer reading first' said the doctor.

'Why?'

'Because if it's too cold over there I'm not going out'.

A brief history of medicine:

2000 BC: Here, eat this root.

1000 AD: That root is heathen. Say this prayer.

1840 AD: That prayer is superstition. Drink this potion.

1940 AD: That potion is a placebo. Swallow this pill.

1985 AD: That pill is ineffective. Take this antibiotic.

20015 AD: That antibiotic is artificial. Here, eat this root.

Journalist (to Harley Street surgeon): 'To what do you attribute your rapid rise in your career?'

Surgeon: 'It has always been my rule never to perform an operation unless I was sure it would be a success either way.'

Patient: 'I'm in so much pain I want to die.'

Doctor: 'You did the right thing to call me.'

A doctor engaged a builder to construct a new path for his house. The doctor went away for three days and when he returned found the builder waiting for his money.

The doctor was not satisfied with his work and said 'Look here — the path is covered with gravel and earth, and in my estimation it's a bad job.'

The builder looked at him in surprise for a moment and replied: 'I'll bet there's many a bad job of yours covered with gravel and earth as well!'

Barrister (to doctor): 'what's the best side to lie on?'

Doctor: 'the side that's paying you!'

My wife had a facelift the other day. They didn't lift it high enough – I can still see it.

'You must give up coffee and — '

'I never drink it, doctor.'

'And stop smoking.'

'I don't smoke.'

'Humph! that's bad. If you haven't anything to give up, I'm afraid I can't do much for you.'

The curator of the museum was classifying Egyptian curios. He observed a perplexed expression on the face of his young assistant.

'What seems to be the matter?' he asked. 'Is there anything you don't understand?'

'Yes, sir,' answered the helper. 'Here is a papyrus on which the characters are so badly traced that they are indecipherable. How shall I classify it?'

'Let me see,' said the curator, examining the piece. 'Just call it a doctor's prescription in the time of Pharaoh.'

Dr Smith: 'How's your new receptionist?'

Dr Jones: 'Highly efficient. I haven't seen a patient all week!'

EDITORS

A well known book publisher, like all editors, was obliged to refuse a great many stories. A lady once wrote to him:

'Dear Sir: you sent back last week a story of mine. I know that you did not read the story, for as a test I glued together pages 18, 19, and 20, and the story came back with these pages still glued; and so I know you are a fraud and turn down stories without reading them.'

The publisher wrote back :

'Madam: At breakfast when I open an egg I don't have to eat the whole egg to discover it is bad.'

Many a man thinks he has become famous when he has merely happened to meet an editor who was hard up for material.

A violinist was bitterly disappointed with the account of his recital printed in the paper of a small town.

'I told your man three or four times,' complained the musician to the owner of the paper, 'that the instrument I used was a genuine Stradivarius, and in his story there was not a word about it, not a word.'

Whereupon the owner said with a laugh: 'That's as it should be. When I start giving out free advertising in my paper, you can let Mr Stradivarius know.'

'Did you read my last novel?' asked the persistent author to the weary literary agent.

'I hope so' came the reply.

The editor of the newspaper in a small town was given an article to print, praising in very elegant language the life and works of a local retired colonel. The colonel and the editor were not the best of friends.

The article came out, but in spelling 'scarred,' in that very important phrase 'battle scarred veteran,' one 'r' was omitted.

The colonel threatened to sue but the editor promised to admit his error in the next issue. In the following issue, in large type, appeared: 'The editor of this paper regrets very much an error in spelling in our last issue. In describing our most worthy colonel, instead of 'battle scared veteran' it should read, 'bottle scarred veteran.' '

What is poetry in motion? The kind that's always going from one editor to another.

Classified Ad Manager: 'Your advertisement begins: "Wanted: Silent Partner."'

Advertiser: 'Yes, that's right.'

Classified Ad Manager: 'Do you want this placed under Business Opportunities or Matrimony?'

ESTATE AGENTS (REALTORS)

'We're calling about the flat advertised.'

'Well, I did mean to let it, but since I've read the estate agent's description of it, I really feel I can't part with it.'

An estate agent who was trying to sell a new block of flats 100 miles from London asked his accountant if he could claim back the tax on his expensive sports car as a legitimate business expense.

'How on earth can a car that cost thirty thousand pounds and which can go 200 miles per hour be a legitimate business expense?' asked the accountant in amazement.

'It's the only way I can honestly claim the flats are 'just 30 minutes drive from London''.

Tenant: 'I'm awfully sorry I can't pay you this month.'

Landlord: 'But that's what you said last month.'

Tenant: 'See – I told you I was a man of my word.'

Smith: 'My landlord has ordered me out because I can't pay my rent.'

Jones: 'Glad I met you. So has mine. Let's change flats.'

GOLF

'Look, dad, I found a lost golf ball in the woods.'

'Are you sure it was lost, Johnny?'

'Oh yes, I saw two golfers looking for it.'

Teacher: 'Johnny, do you know what becomes of boys who use bad language when they're playing marbles?'

Little Johnny: 'Yes, miss. They grow up and play golf.'

Four men were playing golf on a course where the hazard on the ninth hole was a deep ravine.

They drove off. Three went into the ravine and one managed to get his ball over. The three who had dropped into the ravine walked up to have a look. Two of them decided not to try to play their balls out and gave up the hole. The third said he would go down and play out his ball. He disappeared into the deep crevasse. Presently his ball came bobbing out and after a time he climbed up.

'How many strokes?' asked one of his opponents.

'Three.'

'But I heard six.'

'Three of them were echoes!'

IRISHMEN

Boss: 'That customer says that every bottle in that box we sent her was broken. Are you sure you wrote 'This side up, handle with care' on it?'

Seamus: 'Sure I am. An' just in case they didn't see it on the top, oi wrote it on the bottom as well.'

Paddy got a job on a farm in the depths of winter. At the end of every day he had to travel a long way across the fields to pick up his pay from the farmhouse. It was freezing cold and he was fed up with the slow journey, so one day he decided to take a short cut across a frozen lake, despite the large warning sign which said 'DANGER: VERY THIN ICE – KEEP OFF'.

When he was halfway across, the ice cracked and then split into pieces across the whole lake, and Paddy was pitched into the freezing water. Attracted by his shouts for help, a passing motorist on a nearby road stopped to give assistance.

'Sweet Mother o' Mary, throw a rope quick to pull me out, for oi can't swim!'

The motorist was puzzled, and shouted across the lake. 'I haven't got a rope. The water's only up to your chest, why can't you just wade out?'

'Sure and don't be such an idiot!' cried Paddy angrily. 'Dis wather must be eight feet deep, for I'm standin' on top of me tractor!'

'Seamus, I hear you've been fighting', said the priest to his parishioner.

'Tis true I was, fathorr.'

'Don't you remember what the Bible says about turning the other cheek?'

'Yes fathorr, but the other feller hit me on the nose, and I've only got one o' them.'

Paddy was passing a Dublin bookshop and the following sign in the window caught his eye:

ALL THIS WEEK: SOPHOCLES' WORKS FOR TEN POUNDS

'Does he begorrah?' exclaimed the Hibernian. 'How's a feller supposed to earn a living with these immigrants undercuttin' us?'

'Mick, what's that piece of blank paper you have in your hand?' asked Seamus.

'Oh, that's a letter from me wife.'

'How do you mean a letter from your wife? Sure, there's no writing on it.'

'Of course not. Didn't I tell ye we're not on speaking terms?'

An Irishman who was noted for his wit went into a pub and called for a pint of beer. The glass was not full enough for Kelly's satisfaction, so he quietly asked the publican how many barrels of beer he sold in a week.

'Ten,' replied the publican.

'I think,' replied Kelly, 'if yer stand me a pint I could put yez on a plan to sell eleven barrels a week.'

'Agreed,' said the landlord, handing him a pint. 'Now how am I to do it?'

Kelly, taking a big drink at his new pint, winked and said 'Always fill your glasses.'

'The witness claims you were driving at ninety miles an hour', said the magistrate, pointing to the witness box.

'Indeed I was not, sor, and I'll take me oath on that,' replied Seamus defiantly. 'It was him dat was doin' ninety and not me!'

'How can you be so sure?' said the magistrate.

Seamus gave a smile of triumph. 'Because I looked over and saw his speedometer when I passed him!'

An Irishman who was rather too fond of strong drink was asked by the parish priest:

'My son, how do you expect to get into Heaven?'

The man replied: 'Shure, and that's aisy! When I get to the gates of Heaven I'll open the door and shut the door, and open the door and shut the door, an' keep on doing that till St. Peter gets impatient and says, 'For goodness' sake, Mike, either come in or stay out!'

A zealous Irish customs officer was trying to locate several 'moonshine' stills which were known to exist in the remote countryside. The man approached Seamus, saying:

'I'll give you five Euros if you can take me to a private still.'

'Sure an' I will' was Seamus' reply as he pocketed the money. 'Come with me.'

For many weary miles over mountain, bog, and moor they tramped, until they came into view of a barracks. Pointing to a soldier seated on a step inside the square, Seamus said:

'There you are, sor, me brother Mike ; he's been in the army for ten years, and he's a private still.'

Seamus: 'You're workin' terrible hard. How many hods of bricks have yez carried up that ladder today?'

Mick: 'Be quiet man. I'm foolin' the boss. I've carried this same hodful up an' down all day, but he tinks I've been workin.'

Kelly applied for a job loading a ship. At first they said he was too small, but he finally persuaded them to give him a trial. He seemed to be making good, and they gradually increased the size of his load until on the last trip he was carrying a 300-pound anvil under each arm. When he was half-way across the gangplank it broke and the Irishman fell in. With a great splashing and spluttering he came to the surface.

'Trow me a rope will ye!' he shouted to his colleagues, then his head disappeared under the water.

A moment later his head reappeared.

'Trow me a rope, I say!' he shouted again.

Once more he sank. A third time he rose struggling.

'Here!' he spluttered angrily, 'if one of you rotten divils don't hurry up an' trow me a rope I'm goin' to drop one o' these damn tings!'

Seamus was working as a loader for a shooting party in rural Ireland. The group stayed in an old inn that was reputed to be haunted. He slept peacefully enough until two in the morning, when he awoke with an unpleasant feeling of oppression. He raised his head and peered about him. The room was wanly illumined by the full moon, and in that weird, bluish light he thought he discerned a small, misshapen, white hand clasping the rail at the foot of the bed.

'Who the divil's there?' he asked tremulously.

There was no reply. The small white hand did not move.

''Who's there says I!' repeated the Hibernian, his courage returning to him. 'Answer me or I'll shoot, I'm warnin' ye.'

Again there was no reply.

Keeping as still as possible, Seamus cautiously reached for one of the shotguns stacked by his bed, took aim, and fired.

It was at that point that poor Seamus fainted. He'd shot off two of his own toes.

A bank robber was wanted for a series of raids in Ireland. Pretty soon the Garda were on his trail, and Dublin's chief of police put out a 'wanted' poster showing a photo of the crook's real face, followed by three stills from CCTV showing him in different disguises. After a while he called Officer Seamus into his office.

'Any progress on this case?' asked the Chief.

'It's goin' pretty well sor!' beamed Officer Seamus. 'We haven't found the first feller yet but we've managed to arrest the other three.'

Paddy: 'Sure and it's terrible, they've put the bus fares up again.'

Seamus: 'That's good news for me then.'

Paddy: 'How's that?'

Seamus: 'I've just started walking to work instead of takin' the bus to save money, so now I'll be savin' even more!'

LAWYERS

Solicitor (whose celebrity client is thinking of getting a divorce): 'Well, you can get it for about two thousand pounds; everything done quietly and no publicity.'

Celebrity client: 'And how much will the real thing cost, with lots of publicity and everything?'

First lawyer: 'Wonderful news. I've just earned a million pounds.'

Second lawyer: 'Honestly?'

First lawyer: 'How dare you suggest otherwise!'

Jones and Brown got into a quarrel and landed before the local magistrate. Jones, the loser, turning to his opponent in a combative frame of mind, cried:

'I'll see you in the county court!'

'I'll see you in the High Court!' said Brown.

'Then I'll take you to the Crown Court!' said Jones.

'I'll see you in hell!' shouted Brown.

'I'll arrange for my lawyer to meet you' said Jones.

An old lag came up before a judge in court. The judge looked at his records and said:

'You have been before this court before, twelve years ago.'

'Yes yeronner' said the recidivist.

'And who was your lawyer then?'

'You were, yeronner'

'I remember now. And who is your lawyer today?'

'Don't need one, yeronner. I'm going to tell the truth this time.'

Definition of a lawyer: Someone who induces two men to strip for a fight, and then runs off with their clothes.

A lawyer with offices in a large office building recently lost a cuff-link, one of a pair that he greatly prized. Being absolutely certain that he had dropped the link somewhere in the building he posted this notice:

'Lost. A gold cuff-link. The owner will deeply appreciate its immediate return.'

That afternoon, on passing the door on which the notice was posted, he noticed somebody had added a note:

'The finder of the missing cuff-link would greatly appreciate it if the owner would kindly lose the other one.'
Lawyer (to ticket collector on train): 'One hundred pounds to go from London to Birmingham. It's outrageous. A law practice would never get away with prices like that. That's nearly ten pounds a mile.'

Ticket collector: 'Think of it in terms of how much we charge per hour and it won't seem so bad!'

LOVE AND MARRIAGE

'My wife took all my money and then left me.'

'You're lucky. My wife took all my money and she's still here!'

Smith: 'Before my wife and I were married we made an agreement that I should have the final say in all major things, and my wife in all the minor.'

'How has it worked?' asked Jones.

Smith smiled. 'So far,' he replied, 'no major matters have come up.'

Nagging wife: 'Didn't I hear the clock strike two as you came in last night?'

Henpecked husband: 'You did, my dear. It started to strike ten, but I stopped it to keep it from waking vou up.'

'I think my fiance's awful. I asked him if he had to choose between me and a million pounds, which he would take, and he said the million.'

'That's all right. He knew if he had the million you'd be easy.'

If a man's wife is his 'better half', does that mean there's nothing left of him if he remarries?

The curate of a church was endeavouring to teach the significance of white to the children at morning service.

'Why.' said he, 'does a bride wear white at her wedding?'

As no one answered, he explained. 'White,' he said, 'stands for purity and joy, and the wedding-day is the most pure and joyous occasion of a woman's life.'

A small boy queried. 'Why do the men all wear black?'

A well-meaning florist was the cause of much embarrassment to a young man who was in love with a rich and beautiful girl.

It appears that one afternoon she informed the young man that the next day would be her birthday, whereupon the suitor remarked that he would the next morning send her some roses, one rose for each year.

That night he wrote a note to his florist, ordering the delivery of twenty roses for the young woman. The florist himself filled the order, and, thinking to improve on it, said to his assistant:

'Here's an order from young Mr Jones for twenty roses. He's one of my best customers, so I'll throw in ten more for good measure.'

'Jack and I have parted forever.'

'Good gracious! What does that mean?'

'Means that I'll get a huge bunch of flowers in about an hour.'

'Yes,' said the old man to his young visitor, 'I am proud of my girls, and would like to see them comfortably married, and as I have made a little money they will not go penniless to their husbands. There is Sophie, twenty-five years old, and a really good girl. I shall give her £10,000 when she marries. Then comes Caroline, who won't see thirty-five again, and I shall give her £30,000, and the man who takes Elizabeth, who is forty, will have £50,000 with her.'

The young man reflected for a moment and then inquired: 'You haven't one about fifty, have you?'

Father (to suitor): 'I won't have my daughter tied for life to some stupid fool.'

Suitor: 'then don't you think you'd better let me take her off your hands?'

Jilly: 'I don't intend to be married until after I'm thirty.'

Julie: 'And I don't intend to be thirty until after I'm married!'

Married man: 'Cheer up! Plenty more fish in the sea.'

Single man: 'Yes, but the last one took all my bait!'

A couple were celebrating their golden wedding anniversary. The husband stood up and talked about the girls he knew in his youth. It seemed that every time he brought home a girl to meet his mother, his mother didn't like her. Finally, he started searching until he found a girl who not only looked like his mother and acted like his mother, she even sounded like his mother. So he brought her home one night to have dinner, and his father didn't like her.

Fortune teller: 'You wish to know about your future husband?'

Lady: 'No; I wish to know about the past of my present husband for future use.'

'Why have I never married?' the old bachelor said in reply to a leading question.

'Well, once upon a time, in a crowd, I trod on a lady's foot. She turned furiously, beginning, 'You clumsy idiot!'

Then she smiled sweetly and said, 'Oh, I beg your pardon ! I thought you were my husband!'

Chauvinist husband (angrily): 'What! no supper ready? This is the absolute limit! I'm going to a restaurant.'

Wife: 'Wait just five minutes.'

Husband: 'Will it be ready then?'

Wife: 'No, but then I'll go with you.'

Two drunks were ambling homeward at an early hour, after being out nearly all night.

'Doesn't your wife miss you on these occasions?' asked one.

'Not often,' replied the other; 'she can throw pretty straight.'

'What's the matter, old man? You look worried.'

'Well, to be honest with you, I am. You know, I took out some life insurance last Thursday.'

'Yes,' replied the sympathetic friend, 'but what has that to do with the worried expression on your face?'

'Well, the very next day my wife bought a new cook-book.'

Two women were admiring each other's new clothing purchases. One showed off her new silk dress.

Fingering the fabric, she said, 'Just think, all this was made possible by a humble little worm.'

'I know,' said the other. 'I just wish *my* husband was as generous.'

'Do you act toward your wife as you did before you married her?'

'Exactly. I remember just how I used to act when I first fell in love with her. I used to lean over the fence in front of her house and gaze at her shadow on the curtain, afraid to go in.'

'And I act just the same way now when I get home late.'

'My wife is mourning the loss of a ten-thousand-pound diamond necklace.'

'Why don't you advertise a thousand pound reward and no questions asked? '

'Well, I could make good on the thousand, but I don't think my wife could keep to the rest of the deal.'

'My wife's an angel.'

'You're lucky. Mine's still alive.'

'My wife helped make me a millionaire.'

'That's wonderful!

'Not really. I was a billionaire before we met.'

'What are you cutting out of the paper?'

'An item about a man getting a divorce because his wife went through his pockets.'

'What are you going to do with it?'

'Put it in my pocket.'

'Darling,' said the young married man, 'I have to go to Paris on business. It will only take a day or so and I hope you won't miss me too much while I'm gone, but...'

'I won't,' answered his young wife, positively, 'because I'm going with you,'

'I wish you could, dear, but it won't be convenient this time. What would you want to go for, anyhow? I'm going to be too busy to be with you.'

'I have to go. I need clothes.'

'But, darling — you can get all the clothes you want right here in London.'

'Thank you. That's all I wanted.'

Mr. Brown: 'I had a strange dream last night, my dear. I thought I saw another man running off with you.'

Mrs. Brown: 'And what did you say to him?'

Mr. Brown: 'I asked him what he was running for.'

'Now,' said the bridegroom to the bride, when they returned from their honeymoon trip, 'let us have a clear understanding before we settle down to married life. Are you the president or the vice-president of this society?'

'I want to be neither president nor vice-president,' she answered. 'I will be content with a subordinate position.'

49

'What position is that, my dear?'

'Treasurer.'

'My wife certainly makes my salary go a long way.'

'So does mine — so far that none of it ever comes back.'

Husband (newly married): 'Don't you think, love, if I were to smoke in the house, it would spoil the curtains?'

Wife: 'Ah, you are the most unselfish and thoughtful husband in the world; of course it would.'

Husband: 'Well, then, take the curtains down.'

The beautiful young woman interviewed a fortune-teller on the usual subjects.

'Lady,' said the clairvoyant, 'you will visit foreign lands, and the courts of kings and queens. You will conquer all rivals and marry the man of your choice. He will be tall and dark and aristocratic looking.'

'And young?' interrupted the lady.

'Yes, and very rich.'

The beautiful lady grasped the fortune teller's hands and pressed them hard.

'Thank you,' she said. 'Now tell me one thing more. How do I get rid of my present husband?'

For every woman who makes a fool out of a man there is another woman who makes a man out of a fool.

'So you want to marry my daughter, do you?' asked the girl's father of her young man.

'Very much indeed,' replied the youth.

'Can you support a family?'

The young man reflected a moment, and then asked. 'How many of you are there?'

A young man had been 'just friends' with a young lady. After a few months however he plucked up the courage to propose to her.

'Let's get married!' he said.

The young lady sighed. 'Who'd have us?'

He (cautiously): 'Would you say "Yes" if I asked you to marry me?'

She (still more cautiously): 'Would you ask me to marry you if I said I would say "Yes" if you asked me to marry you?'

'Does your husband remember your wedding anniversary?'

'No; so I remind him of it in January and June, and get two presents.'

MONEY

A miser grows rich by seeming poor; an extravagant man grows poor by seeming rich. — Shenstone.

Jenkins was always trying to borrow money, and his friends had begun to avoid him.

One morning he tackled an acquaintance in the street before the latter had a chance to escape.

'I say, old man,' began Jenkins, 'I'm in a terrible fix. I want some money badly, and I haven't the slightest idea where on earth I'm going to get it from.'

'Glad to hear it, my boy,' returned the other promptly. 'I was afraid that you might have an idea you could borrow it from me.'

A story is told of the Duke of Wellington, who once complimented a soldier for an act of gallantry, and asked him which he would prefer: 100 pounds or a medal.

'Would your lordship please tell me the value of the medal?' inquired the private.

'Oh, it is not worth much intrinsically, perhaps two pounds.'

'Then, your lordship, I will take the medal and ninety-eight pounds.'

A miserly millionaire, was approached by a friend who used his most persuasive powers to have him dress more in accordance with his station in life.

'I am surprised, ' said the friend 'that you should let yourself go, and become shabby'

'But I'm not shabby,' firmly interposed the miser.

'Oh, but you are,' returned his old friend. 'Remember your father. He was always neatly, even elaborately, dressed. His clothes were always finely tailored and of the best material.'

'Well then' shouted the miser, triumphantly, 'these clothes I've got on were my father's!'

Old lady (on bus): 'Has anyone here dropped a roll of bank notes, with a rubber band around them?'

'Yes, I have!' cried a dozen at once.

Old lady: 'Well, I've just found the rubber band.'

A workman was busily employed by the roadside, and a nosey passer-by stopped to inquire, 'What are you digging for?' The workman looked up.

'Money,' he replied.

'Money! And when do you expect to strike it, my good man?'

'On payday!'

'What on earth do you mean, winning the lottery helped cure your deafness?'

'As soon as it was in the papers, I heard from my ex-wife.'

'Did you ever realise anything on that investment?'

'Oh, yes.'

'What did you realise on it?'

'What a fool I'd been.'

Librarian (to tramp): Why are you always reading that book on income tax?

Tramp: 'I'm trying to work out how much money I save by not having any.'

'I am going to start growing our own food,' announced a self-sufficiency convert to his wife. 'A few months from now I won't be worrying about prices in the shops.'

'No,' said his wife; 'you'll be wondering how the vegetables so cheaply'.

MOTHERS IN LAW

'I haven't spoken to my mother-in-law for two years. We haven't quarrelled. I just don't like to interrupt her.'

A man was driving with his mother-in-law. A police car overtook, stopped the car and the officer said:

'A woman just fell out of your car two miles back'

'Thank heavens for that,' said the man. 'I thought I'd gone deaf.'

On a family holiday in the Holy Land a man's mother in law died suddenly. He met with the British consul to discuss arrangements for returning the body to England.

'You have two choices,' said the consul. 'You can send the body back to England, which will cost £5000, or I can arrange a local burial which will cost only £200. Which would you prefer?'

The man pondered for a moment and said 'I'll pay the five thousand.'

'That's highly commendable of you, sir. Not many men would have been willing to make such a generous gesture.'

t being generous' said the man. 'It's just that I seem to
~~remember~~ ember a story about someone being buried round here who
~~came~~ he back to life after three days, so I'm taking no chances.'

My mother-in-law is a well balanced person. She's got a chip on
BOTH shoulders.'

Jones noticed an unusual funeral procession going towards the local
cemetery. A man was walking a large dog on a lead. Behind him
were two hearses and behind them, a long procession of men.

Jones approached the man. 'Pardon me, sir, but this is such an
unusual cortege, may I ask what happened?'

'Well,' said the man, as he walked slowly along, 'this dog killed my
wife.' He pointed to the first hearse.

'Then who's in the second hearse?' asked Jones.

'My mother in law. The dog killed her as well.'

Jones thought for a moment then said 'Can I borrow the dog?'

The man pointed behind the hearses. 'Join the queue.'

'Does your mother-in-law visit often?'

'Only twice a year.'

'Lucky you.'

'Not really. She stays six months each time!'

NEIGHBOURS

Boring neighbour: 'I've moved quite close to you now. I'm living just across the river.'

'You must drop in some time.'

'I've just had skylights installed in my ceiling.'

'That sounds nice.'

'They are, but the woman upstairs isn't too happy about them.'

'If I ever win the lottery, my neighbours are going to be rich too.'

'That's very kind of you to remember that old couple next door.'

'I'm not giving them anything — I meant I'll be moving to a rich neighbourhood!'

POLITICIANS

First MP (wearily): 'I suppose I'll be up all night tonight; I have to make out my expense account.'

Second MP (more hopefully): 'Why don't you tell the truth and get a good night's rest?'

Politician (on the platform): 'These are not my figures, ladies and gentlemen; they are the figures of a man who knows what he is talking about.'

Son: 'Dad, what's the future of the verb 'invest'?'

Father (an MP): 'Investigation.'

A newly elected Member of Parliament was watching the Speaker's procession as it wended its way through the lobby of the House of Commons. First came the Speaker, and then the chaplain, and next the other officers.

'Who's that man?' asked the MP to a longstanding member, pointing to the chaplain.

'That is the chaplain of the House,' said the older man.

'Does he pray for the members?' asked the new MP.

'No — when he goes into the House he looks around and sees the members sitting there and then he prays for the country.'

During a parliamentary debate, the Honourable Member for Loamshire called the Honourable Member for Blankshire an ass.

The expression was unparliamentary, and in retraction, the Loamshire MP said:

'While I withdraw the unfortunate word, Mr. Speaker, I must insist that the gentleman from Blankshire is out of order.'

'How am I out of order?' yelled the Blankshire MP.

'You'll have to ask a vet,' answered the other, and that was parliamentary enough to stay on the record.

Definition of a majority: a large number of people who have got tired out trying to think for themselves and have decided to accept somebody else's opinion.'

'Have you made any New Year resolutions or turned over a new leaf or anything like that?'

'No need of them. If I have any lingering vices I feel that I need only wait for the government to introduce legislation that will make them impossible.'

Man (to MP): you promised me a job.'

MP: 'But there are no jobs.'

Man: 'I need a job.'

MP: 'Well, I'll ask for a commission to investigate why there are no jobs and you can get a job on that.'

Teacher: 'What is another name for the Mother of Parliaments?'

Little Johnny: 'Mrs Parliaments?'

PUBLIC SPEAKING

'Do you know what it is to go before an audience?'

'No. I spoke before an audience once, but most of it went before I did.'

Chairman (at business dinner): 'Ladies and gentlemen, before I introduce the next speaker, there will be a short break, giving you all a chance to go out and stretch your legs.'

Guest: 'Who is the next speaker?'

Chairman: 'Before telling you who he is, I would rather wait until you come back.'

A story is told of a well known actor with a fondness for the bottle and his agent attending a dinner where the actor was due to give a speech before royalty. Despite being a seasoned performer, he was nervous about speaking to such distinguished guests.

The actor said to his agent: 'I want you to start the laughter and applause. Every time I take a drink of water, you applaud; and every time I wipe my forehead with my handkerchief, you laugh.'

The agent thought for a moment and said, 'You'd better change the signals. I'm more likely to burst out laughing when I see you deliberately take a drink of water.'

RELIGION

Brown (on sinking lifeboat): 'Men, the boat is sinking! Is there any one here who knows how to pray?'

Jones (eagerly): 'I do.'

Brown: 'All right. You pray and the rest of us will put on life jackets. There's one short.'

RE teacher: 'Can anyone tell me who caused 'the Writing on the Wall'?

Little Johnny: 'Please sir, it wasn't me!'

It was the week before little Johnny's birthday, and he was on his knees at his bedside praying for presents in a very loud voice.

'Please send me,' he shouted, 'a bicycle, a cricket bat, a football...'

'What are you praying so loud for?' his younger brother interrupted. 'God isn't deaf.'

'I know he isn't,' said little Johnny, winking toward the next room, 'but granny is.'

The teacher had asked, 'Why did David say he would rather be a door-keeper in the house of the Lord?'

'Because,' answered a boy, 'he could then walk outside while the sermon was being preached.'

A visitor to a small Welsh town which had four chapels, none of which were well attended, asked a pillar of one poor dying congregation, 'How's your chapel getting on?' 'Not very well, look you,' said Jones, 'but, thank the Lord, the others are not doing any better.'

'Are you a pillar of the church?'

'No, I'm a flying buttress -I support it from the outside.'

A bus driver and a priest from a mountainous Italian village both died at the same time, and appeared before the Pearly Gates. St Peter allowed the bus driver in, but told the priest there was no vacancy. The priest protested.

'But I'm a man of God – how can you keep me out and let that bus driver in? He was drunk half the time he drove round those mountain bends!'

'Well,' said St Peter, 'in your church everybody used to fall asleep. But as soon as they were in his bus, everybody used to start praying!'

If the tabloid press had existed in Biblical times, after Jesus walked on water the headlines would have read 'SON OF GOD CAN'T SWIM.'

At a formal dinner, a businessman was boasting of his worldly success to a bishop. The bishop listened politely, then said:

'My good man, all this is most interesting – but I hope that you give thanks to your Creator for it.'

'I certainly do,' replied the businessman. 'I'm a self-made man!'

SCIENCE

A scientist was enthusiastically telling a sceptical layman about his chemical research.

'We are searching for a universal solvent - something that will dissolve all things,' said the chemist.

'What good will that be?'

'Just imagine! It will dissolve all things. If we want a solution of iron, glass, gold -anything, all that we have to do is to drop it in this solution.'

'Fine,' said the sceptic, 'fine! Just one question – what are you going to keep it in?'

The driver of a famous scientist used to sit at the back of the hall during each of his lectures, and after a period of time, remarked to the scientist that he could probably give the lecture himself, having heard it several times. So at the next stop on the tour, the scientist and the driver swapped places, with the scientist sitting at the back, in driver's uniform. The driver gave the lecture, flawlessly. At the end, a member of the audience asked a difficult question. Thinking quickly, the driver replied:

'The answer to that question is quite simple, I bet that even my driver, sitting up at the back, there, could answer it...'

A mosquito was heard to complain
That chemists had poisoned her brain.
The cause of her sorrow
Was para-dichloro-diphenyl-trichloroethane.

In the period that Einstein was active as a professor, one of his students came to him and said: 'The questions of this year's exam are the same as last year's!' 'True, Einstein said, 'but this year all answers are different.'

Old chemistry teachers never die, they just fail to react.

Mathmetician: the glass is half full
Physicist: the glass is half empty
Engineer: the glass is too big

Albert Einstein, who fancied himself as a violinist, was rehearsing a Haydn string quartet. When he failed for the fourth time to get his entry in the second movement, the cellist looked up and said, 'The problem with you, Albert, is that you simply can't count.'

When Gladstone met Michael Faraday, he asked him whether his work on electricity would be of any use.

'Yes, sir' remarked Faraday with prescience, 'One day you will tax it.'

After a lecture on the solar system, philosopher William James was approached by a determined elderly lady with a theory.

'We don't live on a ball rotating around the sun,' she said. 'We live on a crust of earth on the back of a giant turtle.'

James decided to be gentle. 'If your theory is correct, madam, what does this turtle stand on?'

'The first turtle stands on the back of a second, far larger turtle, of course.'

'But what does this second turtle stand on?'

The old lady crowed triumphantly. 'It's no use, Mr. James - it's turtles all the way down!'

SCOTSMEN

After discovering that they had won 10 million pounds in the lottery, McTavish and his wife sat down to discuss their future. Mrs McTavish announced:

'After twenty years of washing other people's stairs, I can throw my old scrubbing brush away at last.'

McTavish nodded in agreement.

'Of course you can, dearie. We can easily afford to buy you a new one now.'

McTavish was observed stripping the wallpaper from his front room.

'Redecorating?' asked a neighbour.

'No, moving house.'

Instead of his usual donation of a penny, McTavish accidentally put a ten pence piece in the collection plate at the Kirk one Sunday.

The steward noticed the mistake, and in silence he passed by McTavish without offering the plate to him for nine more Sundays.

On the tenth Sunday, McTavish ignored the plate as usual, but the steward this time announced in a loud voice:

'Yer time's up, McTavish.'

McTavish asked the bus driver how much it would cost to travel into the centre of Glasgow.

'A poond' said the driver.

McTavish was shocked and decided to run after the bus for a few stops.

'How much noo?' he asked.

'Still a poond'.

McTavish ran after the bus for another three stops and, panting, he asked

'How much noo?'

The driver smiled and replied 'one poond fifty. Ye're runnin' the wrang way!'

A Londoner moved to Scotland and wasn't impressed by the size of the mountains.

'What's so great about them?' asked the southerner of a local farmer. 'I could climb that one in a day,' he said, pointing to the rising peak ahead of him on the path.

'I don't know aboot that' responded the farmer, 'a young couple went up this path last year and never came back.'

The Londoner suddenly looked fearful. 'Oh! Were they lost?'

'Naw,' was the reply, 'they went doon the other side!'

McTavish was passing through a small highland town and knocked on the door of the manse.

'Minister, ye did me a favour ten years ago,' said McTavish, 'and I have nivver forgotten it.'

'Ah,' replied the good man with a holy expression on his face, 'and you have come back to repay me?'

'Not exactly,' replied McTavish. 'I've just got into toon and need another favour, and I thought of you right away.'

McTavish: 'An' so ye leave Glesga' on Monday. What are ye daein the morrow nicht?'

McDougal: 'Tomorrow, Thursday, I've no plans.'

McTavish: 'An' the next nicht?'

McDougal: 'I'm free then, too.'

McTavish: 'An' what will ye be daein on the Saturday?'

McDougal: 'On Saturday ah'm havin' dinner wi' the McPhersons.'

McTavish: 'What a pity! Aa wanted ye to take dinner wi'us on Saturday!'

Two old Scotsmen sat by the roadside, talking and puffing away merrily at their pipes.

'There's no much pleasure in smokin', Sandy,' said Donald.

'Hoo dae ye mak' that oot?' questioned Sandy.

'Weel,' said Donald, 'ye see, if ye're smokin' yer ain bacca ye're thinkin' o' the awfu' expense, an' if ye're smokin' some ither body's, yer pipe's packed sae tight it willnae draw.'

A Scotsman had been presented with a pint bottle of rare old Scotch whisky. He was walking briskly along the road toward home, when along came a car which he did not side step quite in time. It threw him down and hurt his leg quite badly. He got up and limped down the road. Suddenly he noticed that something warm and wet was trickling down his leg.

'Oh, God,' he groaned, 'I hope that's blood!'

A newly appointed Scots minister on his first Sunday of office had reason to complain of the poorness of the collection.

'Mon,' replied one of the elders, 'they are close - verra close.'

'But,' confidentially, 'the auld meenister he put three or four pennies intae the plate hissel', just to gie them a start. Of course he took the pennies awa' with him afterward.'

The new minister tried the same plan, but the next Sunday he again had to report a dismal failure. The total collection was not only small, but he was grieved to find that his own pennies were missing.

'Ye may be a better preacher than the auld meenister,' exclaimed the elder, 'but if ye had half the knowledge o' the world, an' o' yer ain flock in particular, ye'd ha' done what he did an' glued the pennies tae the plate.'

Sandy McDougal sat with his girlfriend Maggie on the sofa.

'A penny for your thochts, Sandy,' murmured Maggie, after a silence of an hour and a half.

'Weel,' replied Sandy slowly, with surprising boldness, 'tae tell ye the truth, I was jist thinkin' how fine it wad be if ye were tae gie me a wee bit kiss.'

'I've nae objection,' simpered Maggie, and kissed him.

Sandy relapsed into a brown study once more, and the clock ticked twenty-seven minutes.

'An' what are ye thinkin' about noo; anither, eh?'

'Nae, nae, lassie; it's a mair serious matter ah'm thinking of the noo.'

'Is it, laddie?' asked Maggie softly. Her heart was going pit-a-pat with expectation.

'An' what micht it be?'

'I was jist thinkin',' answered Sandy, 'that it was aboot time ye were paying me that penny!

SHOPPING

Customer: 'What! Five hundred pounds for that antique? Last week you said three hundred and fifty.'

Dealer: 'Yes, I know; but the cost of labour and materials has gone up!'

'How much are those pineapples?'

'Two for a pound.'

'How much for one?'

'Seventy pence.'

'I'll take the other one.'

'I wish to make a complaint. This vinegar's got lumps in it.'

'Madam, those are pickled onions.'

'Darling,' said the young husband as he took the bottle of milk from the fridge and held it up to the light, 'have you noticed that there's never cream on this milk?'

'I spoke to the man at the shop about it,' she replied, 'and he explained that the company always fill their bottles so full that there's no room for cream on top.'

Customer in bookshop: 'I'm looking for *The Letters of Charles Lamb*.'

New assistant: 'Have you tried the post office?'

Customer in shoe shop: 'I'm afraid these Louis XV heels are a bit high for me. Do you have anything a bit smaller, like a Louis X?'

In a busy department store, a lady asked to see coats. After the assistant had emptied the shelves and piled the counters with blankets of every description and colour, the lady thanked him and said:

'I was just looking for a friend.'

'Well, madam,' said the obliging assistant, 'if you think your friend is among these coats, I'll look again.'

Little Johnny stood beside his mother as she made her selection from the health food shop, and the latter told the boy to take a handful of nuts, but the child shook his head.

'What's the matter, don't you like nuts?' asked the shopkeeper.

'Yes,' replied Little Johnny.

'Then go ahead and take some.'

Little Johnny hesitated, but the shopkeeper put a generous handful in Johnny's pocket.

Outside the shop his mother asked: 'Why didn't you take the nuts when he told you to?'

Little Johnny winked as he said: "Cause his hand was bigger than mine.'

Two rival butchers had shops on opposite sides of a high street, and, one day, one of them placed over his shop a sign saying :

'Sausages sold to the nobility of the county.'

The next day, over the way, appeared the sign: 'Sausages sold to the nobility of the whole country.'

Not to be outdone, the rival put up what he evidently regarded as a final statement, namely: 'Sausages sold to the Queen.'

Next day there appeared over the door of the first sausagemaker the simple expression of loyalty: 'God save the Queen.'

A shopkeeper put a box outside his shop one day, labelled 'For the Blind.' A few weeks afterwards the box disappeared.

'What's happened to your box for the blind?' he was asked.

'Oh, I got enough money,' he replied. 'And,' pointing upward to the new canvas blind that sheltered his shop-window, 'there's the blind.'

Definition of luxuries: things that were necessities two years ago.

TAXIS

''Ere, Jim,' said the friend of the cab driver, standing in front of the vehicle, 'there's a wallet lying on the floor of your taxi.'

The driver looked carefully around and then whispered:

'Sometimes when business is bad I put it there and leave the door open. It's empty, but you've no idea how many people'll jump in for a short drive when they see it.'

'How much to the station?'

'Ten pounds.'

'How much for the luggage?'

'Luggage is free.'

'In that case take the bags for me and I'll walk.'

An English visitor to New York got into a taxi. The driver, who did not speak much English, jumped a red light. The Englishman was shocked and exclaimed to the cabbie:

'You just jumped a red light!'

'Relax,' said the driver. 'My brudder, he always drive taxi like this.'

Pretty soon the cab came to another red light and once more, the driver speeded up and shot through it. The Englishman complained again, but once more the driver just smiled and said:

'Relax, my brudder, he always drive taxi like this!'

Eventually they came to a green light, and this time the driver jammed on the brakes and stopped the cab.

'What now?' exclaimed the Englishman in confusion.

The driver looked worried. 'I think my brudder coming the other way.'

TEACHERS

Father (reading report card): 'Who is the laziest person in your class, Johnny?'

Little Johnny: 'I don't know, dad.'

Father: 'I should think you should know. When all the others are studying hard or doing their exercises, who is it sits idly in his seat and watches the rest, instead of working himself?'

Little Johnny: 'The teacher.'

By way of enlarging the children's vocabulary, a primary school teacher was in the habit of giving her class a certain word and asking them to form a sentence in which that word occurred. One day she gave the class the word 'notwithstanding.'

There was a pause, and then a bright-faced youngster held up his hand.

'Well, what is your sentence, Johnny?' asked the teacher.

'Dad wore his trousers out, but notwithstanding.'

Little Johnny: 'Dad!'

Father (sighing): 'Yes?'

Little Johnny: 'Teacher says we're here to help others.'

Father: 'Of course we are.'

Little Johnny: 'Well, what are the others here for?'

We have just learnt of a teacher who started with nothing twenty years ago and who has retired with the comfortable fortune of two hundred thousand pounds. This was acquired through industry, economy, conscientious effort, indomitable perseverance, and the death of an uncle who left her an estate valued at £199,999.50.

Little Johnny: 'Dad, would you be glad if I saved you five pounds?'

Father: 'Certainly, my son.'

Little Johnny: 'Well, you said if I brought a first-class report from my teacher this week you would give me five pounds, and I didn't bring it.'

One day Little Johnny's teacher asked him if he was going on the school outing.

'No,' replied the young philosopher, 'I ain't going.'

'No Johnny,' said the teacher, 'you must not say, "I ain't going." You must say, "I am not going."' And he proceeded to give him a little lesson in grammar: 'You are not going. He is not going. We are not going. You are not going. They are not
going.' Now, can you say all that?'

'Of course I can,' responded Little Johnny enthusiastically. 'There ain't nobody going.'

'What is the plural of man, Johnny?' asked the teacher of the small pupil.

'Men,' answered Little Johnny.

'And, the plural of child?'

'Twins!'

Teacher: 'A fool can ask more questions than a wise man can answer.'

Pupil: 'No wonder so many of us fail our exams!'

Teacher: 'Johnny, your face is clean, but how did your hands get so dirty?'

Little Johnny: 'From washing my face.'

The teacher was delivering the final lesson of the term. He dwelt with much emphasis on the fact that each pupil should devote all of the following weekend to preparing for the final examinations.

'The examination papers are now in the hands of the printer. Are there
any questions to be asked?'

A hand shot up.

'Yes sir. Who's the printer?'

TRAMPS

Lady (to tramp): 'Out of work, are you? Then you're just in time. I've got some firewood to be chopped up and I was just going to send for a man to do it.'

Tramp: 'Where does he live? I'll go and get him.'

'I saw a tramp the other day asleep in a doorway with a sign in front of him saying: "Please help: one day it could be you"'

'I hope you gave him something?'

'No, I took the sign, just in case he's right.'

Tramp (to millionaire): 'Spare ten pence for a cup of tea, guv?'

Millionaire: 'Here you are, my good man.'

Tramp: 'Thanks guv, but why are you following me?'

Millionaire: 'I want to find out where you can get a cup of tea for ten pence.'

UNIONS

In the Great War an aristocratic British officer and his men were surrounded in No Man's Land by German soldiers. The British began fighting fiercely, but after a few minutes of firing, one Tommy, who was a shop steward in civilian life, sat down and did nothing.

'Are you mad, man?' shouted the officer. 'Why have you stopped shooting? We're outnumbered four to one'.

'Well I've killed my four' came the reply.

A road crew foreman called into the shop.

Foreman: 'we have a problem.'

Boss: 'What's wrong?'

Foreman: 'we forgot our shovels.'

Boss: 'I'll be out there as quick as I can. Lean on each other until I get there.'

In the 1970s a Russian trade delegation visited a British factory to analyse capitalist methods.

'What time do your men start work in morning?' asked the Russian to the factory owner. '9' o'clock', said the owner.

'Pah!' replied the Russian. 'In Russia, factory worker start at 6 o'clock! How long is lunch break?'

'One hour,' said the owner.

Pah!' replied the Russian. 'In Russia, lunch break is ten minutes! What time men go home?'

'5 o'clock,' replied the owner.

'Pah!' shouted the Russian. 'In Russia, men never go home before 10 o'clock!'

Slightly exasperated, the owner replied, 'My good man, you'd never get the unions here to accept that.'

'Why not?' demanded the Russian.

'Because they're all communists!'

USA

A party of tourists were looking at Vesuvius in full eruption.

'Ain't this just like hell!' exclaimed an American.

'Ah, these Americans,' said the Italian guide to himself, 'where have they not been?'

Sir Walter Raleigh was called to take a cup of tea with Queen Elizabeth.

'It was very good of you, Sir Walter,' said her Majesty, smiling sweetly upon the gallant Knight, 'to ruin your cloak the other day so that my feet should not be wet by that horrid puddle. May I not instruct my Lord High Treasurer to reimburse you for it?'

'Don't mention it, your Majesty,' replied Raleigh. 'It only cost two shillings and sixpence, but I have already sold it to an American collector for eight thousand pounds.'

Other titles from Montpelier Publishing
Available from Amazon

Frugal living and moneysaving
1001 Ways to Save Money
A Treasury of Thrift
The Men's Guide to Frugal Grooming
The Frugal Gentleman

Body, mind and spirit
Non-Religious Wedding Readings
The Simple Living Companion
Non-Religious Funeral Readings
Spiritual Readings for Funerals
Marriage Advice

Humour and puzzles
The Book of Church Jokes
After Dinner Laughs 2
Scottish Jokes
The Bumper Book of Riddles, Puzzles and Rhymes
Wedding Jokes

Travel
The Dalai Lama Next Door
The Slow Bicycle Companion

Men's interest
The Pipe Smoker's Companion
Advice to Gentlemen
The Real Ale Companion
The Cigar Collection

Printed in Great Britain
by Amazon